BAD DAD
JOKES

MW00397681

© 2018, 2022 Willow Creek Press

All Rights Reserved. No part of this book may be reproduced or transmitted in any form by any means, electronic or mechanical, including photocopying, recording, or by any information storage and retrieval system, without written permission from the publisher.

Published by Willow Creek Press, Inc.
P.O. Box 147, Minocqua, Wisconsin 54548

Printed in the United States

BAD DAD JOKES

OVER 300 OF THE "BEST OF THE WORST" DAD JOKES OF ALL TIME.

WILLOW CREEK PRESS®

WHAT DO YOU CALL
A GUY WITH A
RUBBER TOE?

ROBERTO.

WHY COULDN'T
THE BICYCLE
STAND UP?

BECAUSE IT WAS
TWO TIRED!

WHAT DO COMPUTERS
EAT FOR A SNACK?

MICROCHIPS.

WHAT'S THE BEST
THING ABOUT
SWITZERLAND?

I DON'T KNOW,
BUT THE FLAG
IS A BIG PLUS.

WHY DO
HUMMINGBIRDS HUM?

BECAUSE THEY DON'T
KNOW THE WORDS.

IF A CHILD REFUSES
TO TAKE A NAP, IS HE
RESISTING A REST?

DID YOU HEAR ABOUT
THE ITALIAN CHEF
THAT DIED?

HE PASTA WAY.

HOW DO YOU MAKE
A TISSUE DANCE?

PUT A LITTLE
BOOGIE IN IT.

HOW DO SNAILS
FIGHT?

THEY SLUG IT OUT.

I WAS THINKING
ABOUT MOVING
TO MOSCOW...

BUT THERE'S NO
POINT IN RUSSIAN
INTO THINGS.

CAN A MATCH BOX?

NO, BUT A TIN CAN.

WHICH SIDE OF A
DUCK HAS THE
MOST FEATHERS?

THE OUTSIDE.

WHY DID THE
PAINTING GO
TO JAIL?

IT WAS FRAMED.

WHAT DO YOU CALL
A PILE OF CATS?

A MEOWTAIN.

WHAT DID THE
BANANA SAY TO
THE DOCTOR?

"I'M NOT
PEELING WELL."

WHERE DO
EGGPLANTS
COME FROM?

CHICKEN PLANTS.

HOW DO BIRDS FLY?

THEY JUST WING IT.

WHY ARE
HAIRDRESSERS
NEVER LATE
FOR WORK?

BECAUSE THEY KNOW
ALL THE SHORT CUTS.

WHAT DO YOU CALL
A GIRL WHO'S JUST
COME BACK FROM
THE BEACH?

SANDY.

WHERE DID THE COW
TAKE HIS DATE?

THE MOOOVIES.

WHAT DO YOU CALL
A MAN WHO
CAN'T STAND?

NEIL.

WHAT DID THE
SCHIZOPHRENIC
BOOKKEEPER SAY?

I HEAR INVOICES.

WHAT DID THE BABY
CORN SAY TO THE
MAMA CORN?

WHERE'S POP CORN?

WHAT DOES A
NUT SAY WHEN
IT SNEEZES?

CASHEW.

HOW DO YOU
ORGANIZE A
SPACE PARTY?

YOU PLANET.

WHAT GOES UP
WHEN THE
RAIN COMES DOWN?

AN UMBRELLA.

WHAT DO YOU
CALL A PIG THAT
DOES KARATE?

A PORK CHOP.

HOW DOES A RANCHER
KEEP TRACK OF
HIS CATTLE?

WITH A COW-CULATOR.

WHAT WAS LUDWIG
VAN BEETHOVEN'S
FAVORITE FRUIT?

BA-NA-NA-NA.

WHAT DO YOU CALL A
T-REX THAT'S BEEN
BEATEN UP?

DINO-SORE.

WHAT DID THE BEAVER
SAY TO THE TREE?

IT'S BEEN NICE
GNAWING YOU.

WHY DIDN'T THE
SAILORS PLAY CARDS?

BECAUSE THE
CAPTAIN
WAS ON DECK.

WHAT DO YOU DO
WITH A SICK BOAT?

TAKE IT TO THE DOC.

THIS GRAVEYARD LOOKS
OVERCROWDED.

PEOPLE MUST BE DYING
TO GET IN THERE!

WHAT DO CATS EAT
FOR BREAKFAST?

MICE KRISPIES.

WHEN THE SMOG
LIFTS IN LOS
ANGELES, WHAT
HAPPENS?

UCLA.

HAVE YOU HEARD ABOUT
THE NEW RESTAURANT
ON THE MOON?

THE FOOD WAS GREAT,
BUT THERE WAS
NO ATMOSPHERE.

THE ENERGIZER
BUNNY WAS ARRESTED
ON A CHARGE
OF BATTERY.

WHAT IS A TREE'S
FAVORITE DRINK?

ROOT BEER.

WHY COULDN'T
DRACULA'S WIFE GET
TO SLEEP?

BECAUSE OF HIS COFFIN.

WHAT DID THE LEFT EYE
SAY TO THE RIGHT EYE?

BETWEEN YOU AND ME
SOMETHING SMELLS.

WHAT DOES MILEY
CYRUS EAT FOR
CHRISTMAS DINNER?

ROAST TWERKY.

WHY DID THE
CHICKEN CROSS
THE PLAYGROUND?

TO GET TO THE
OTHER SLIDE.

I GAVE ALL MY DEAD
BATTERIES AWAY TODAY...

FREE OF CHARGE.

MY BOSS TOLD
ME TO HAVE A
GOOD DAY...

SO I WENT HOME.

HOW DO YOU GET 500
OLD COWS IN A BARN?

PUT UP A BINGO SIGN.

WHY WOULDN'T THE
SHRIMP SHARE HIS
TREASURE?

BECAUSE HE WAS
A LITTLE SHELLFISH.

WHICH WINTER MONTH
DO PEOPLE SLEEP
THE LEAST?

FEBRUARY.

WHY DID THE
ELEPHANTS KEEP
GETTING KICKED OUT
OF THE POOL?

THEY KEPT DROPPING
THEIR TRUNKS!

HOW DO YOU MAKE AN
OCTOPUS LAUGH?

WITH TEN-TICKLES

I DIDN'T LIKE MY
BEARD AT FIRST...

THEN IT GREW ON ME.

HOW CAN YOU GET
FOUR SUITS FOR
A DOLLAR?

BUY A DECK OF CARDS.

WHAT DID THE MAMA
COW SAY TO THE
BABY COW?

"IT'S PASTURE
BEDTIME."

WHAT HAPPENS IF A FROG
PARKS ILLEGALLY?

THEY GET TOAD.

WHAT DO CARS EAT
ON THEIR TOAST?

TRAFFIC JAM.

WHERE DO BEEF
BURGERS GO
TO DANCE?

THE MEATBALL.

WHAT DO YOU DO IF
ATTACKED BY A CLAN
OF CLOWNS?

GO FOR THE
JUGGLER.

WHY SHOULDN'T YOU
GIVE ELSA A BALLOON?

BECAUSE SHE'LL
LET IT GO.

HOW DO YOU FIX
A CABBAGE?

WITH A CABBAGE
PATCH.

I DON'T PLAY SOCCER
BECAUSE I ENJOY
THE SPORT.

I'M JUST DOING IT
FOR KICKS!

WHAT DID THE
LAWYER NAME HIS
DAUGHTER?

SUE.

WHY IS A
RIVER RICH?

IT HAS BANKS
ON BOTH SIDES.

WHY CAN'T YOU
TRUST AN ATOM?

BECAUSE THEY MAKE
UP EVERYTHING.

WHAT'S
FORREST
GUMP'S
PASSWORD?

1FOREST1.

A BLIND MAN WALKS
INTO A BAR...

AND A TABLE.
AND A CHAIR.

WHY IS PETER PAN
ALWAYS FLYING?

HE NEVERLANDS.

WHY COULDN'T
THE LEOPARD PLAY
HIDE AND SEEK?

BECAUSE HE WAS
ALWAYS SPOTTED.

HOW DID THE
HIPSTER BURN
HIS MOUTH?

HE ATE PIZZA BEFORE
IT WAS COOL.

WHAT'S BROWN
AND STICKY?

A STICK.

WHY DON'T THEY
PLAY POKER IN
THE JUNGLE?

TOO MANY
CHEETAHS.

WHAT TYPE OF BOOK HAS
ONLY CHARACTERS AND
NO STORY?

A TELEPHONE BOOK.

SPRING IS HERE...

I'M SO EXCITED I
WET MY PLANTS!

HAVE YOU HEARD THE
STORY OF THE MAGIC
SANDWICH?

NEVERMIND, IT'S JUST A
BUNCH OF BOLOGNA.

WHY IS THE
BARN SO NOISY?

BECAUSE THE
COWS HAVE HORNS.

WHAT DID THE CAKE
SAY TO THE FORK?

WANT A PIECE OF ME?

WHAT DO YOU CALL A
BEAR WITH NO TEETH?

A GUMMY BEAR.

WHAT'S THE DIFFERENCE
BETWEEN A POORLY
DRESSED MAN ON
A TRICYCLE AND A
WELL DRESSED MAN
ON A BICYCLE?

ATTIRE!

WHEN ARE
HOLES BEAUTIFUL?

WHEN THEY'RE GORGES.

WHAT DID ONE HAT SAY
TO ANOTHER?

YOU STAY HERE,
I'LL GO ON A HEAD.

WHAT DO YOU
CALL A DINOSAUR
WITH AN EXTENSIVE
VOCABULARY?

A THESAURUS.

HOW MANY LIPS DOES
A FLOWER HAVE?

TU-LIPS.

NURSE: "THE INVISIBLE MAN IS HERE FOR HIS APPOINTMENT."

DOCTOR: "TELL HIM I'M SORRY I CAN'T SEE HIM RIGHT NOW."

MY DOCTOR SAID I HAD TYPE A BLOOD...

BUT IT WAS A TYPE O.

WHEN IS A DOOR NOT A DOOR?

WHEN IT'S AJAR.

WHAT'S A SHARK'S
FAVORITE SANDWICH?

PEANUT BUTTER
AND JELLYFISH.

THE PAST, PRESENT,
AND FUTURE WALKED
INTO A BAR...

IT WAS TENSE.

HOW DO YOU MAKE
THE NUMBER
SEVEN EVEN?

DROP THE "S."

WHERE DO YOU
LEARN HOW TO
MAKE ICE CREAM?

SUNDAE SCHOOL.

WHAT'S HARRY POTTER'S WAY
TO GET TO THE BOTTOM
OF A HILL?

RUNNING... JK! ROLLING.

WHAT DO YOU
SAY TO A LOLLIPOP
WHEN YOU THROW
IT AWAY?

"SO LONG SUCKER!"

WHAT DO YOU CALL A
DUCK THAT STEALS?

A ROBBER DUCK.

PEOPLE ARE
MAKING TOO MANY
APOCALYPSE JOKES...

IT'S LIKE THEY
THINK THERE'S
NO TOMORROW.

WHAT DOES A CLAM
DO ON ITS BIRTHDAY?

SHELLABRATE!

WANNA HEAR A JOKE
ABOUT A STONE?

NEVERMIND, I WILL
JUST SKIP THAT ONE.

IT LOOKS LIKE
MY CAT'S SICK...

HE DOESN'T SEEM
TO BE FELINE WELL.

HOW DO YOU GET
A BABY ALIEN
TO SLEEP?

YOU ROCKET.

WHAT IS TALL WHEN IT
IS YOUNG AND SHORT
WHEN IT IS OLD?

A CANDLE.

HOW DO YOU TURN
WHITE CHOCOLATE
INTO DARK
CHOCOLATE?

TURN OFF THE LIGHT.

WHAT DID THE
BLANKET SAY AS IT
FELL OFF THE BED?

OH SHEET!

DID YOU HEAR ABOUT
THE TWO GUYS THAT
STOLE A CALENDAR?

THEY EACH GOT
SIX MONTHS.

WHY DID THE MAN
NAME HIS DOGS
ROLEX AND TIMEX?

BECAUSE THEY
WERE WATCH DOGS.

HOW DO BILLBOARDS
TALK?

SIGN LANGUAGE.

WHY DIDN'T THE
MELONS GET
MARRIED?

BECAUSE THEY
CANTALOUPE.

WHAT KIND OF SHOES
DO NINJAS WEAR?

SNEAKERS.

WHY DID CINDERELLA
FAIL AT BASKETBALL?

BECAUSE SHE
HAD A PUMPKIN
FOR A COACH.

WHY DID THE
ARCHAEOLOGIST'S
WIFE DIVORCE HIM?

BECAUSE HE WAS
CARBON DATING.

WHAT DID ONE
TOILET SAY TO THE
OTHER TOILET?

YOU LOOK A
BIT FLUSHED.

HOW DID THE
FROG DIE?

HE KERMIT SUICIDE.

BEING AN ASTRONAUT
IS FUNNY...

IT'S THE ONLY JOB WHERE
YOU GET FIRED BEFORE
YOU START WORK.

WHAT DID THE MATH
BOOK SAY TO ITS
THERAPIST?

I'VE GOT A LOT
OF PROBLEMS.

WHAT DO YOU CALL A
FISH WITH NO EYES?

A FSH.

WHY ARE FISH
EASY TO WEIGH?

BECAUSE THEY HAVE
THEIR OWN SCALES.

WHAT'S THE LAST THING
THAT GOES THROUGH A
BUG'S MIND AS IT HITS
YOUR WINDSHIELD?

IT'S BUTT.

HOW DO YOU FIX A
BROKEN TUBA?

WITH A TUBA GLUE.

WHAT DID ONE
OCEAN SAY TO
ANOTHER OCEAN?

NOTHING. IT
JUST WAVED.

I'M READING A BOOK
ABOUT ANTI-GRAVITY...

IT'S IMPOSSIBLE
TO PUT DOWN.

WHERE DO YOU FIND A
COW WITH NO LEGS?

RIGHT WHERE
YOU LEFT IT.

WHY DOES A MILKING
STOOL ONLY HAVE
3 LEGS?

BECAUSE THE COW
HAS THE UTTER.

DID YOU HEAR ABOUT
THE GUY WHO DRANK
8 COKES?

HE BURPED 7UP.

WHAT DO YOU CALL
AN EXPLOSIVE
HORSE?

NEIGH-PALM.

WHAT DID THE
MOUNTAIN CLIMBER
NAME HIS SON?

CLIFF.

WHAT HAS MORE
LIVES THAN A CAT?

A FROG BECAUSE
IT CROAKS
EVERY NIGHT.

WHAT DO YOU CALL A
SLEEPWALKING NUN?

A ROAMIN' CATHOLIC.

WHAT'S THE DIFFERENCE
BETWEEN A GUITAR
AND A FISH?

YOU CAN TUNE A GUITAR,
BUT YOU CAN'T TUNA FISH.

WHY DID THE CAT RUN
AWAY FROM THE TREE?

BECAUSE OF ITS BARK.

WHAT DO YOU
CALL AN APOLOGY
WRITTEN IN DOTS
AND DASHES?

A REMORSE CODE.

IF YOU HAVE 13
APPLES IN ONE HAND
AND 10 ORANGES IN
THE OTHER, WHAT
DO YOU HAVE?

BIG HANDS.

TODAY AT THE BANK,
AN OLD LADY ASKED
ME TO HELP CHECK
HER BALANCE...

SO I PUSHED
HER OVER.

THE ROTATION OF EARTH
REALLY MAKES MY DAY.

I KNOW A LOT OF JOKES
ABOUT UNEMPLOYED
PEOPLE...

BUT NONE OF
THEM WORK.

CAN A KANGAROO JUMP
HIGHER THAN A HOUSE?

OF COURSE, A HOUSE
DOESN'T JUMP AT ALL.

WHY AREN'T KOALAS
ACTUAL BEARS?

THE DON'T MEET THE
KOALAFICATIONS.

WHY DID THE
RUNNER STOP
LISTING TO MUSIC?

BECAUSE SHE BROKE
TOO MANY RECORDS.

DID YOU HEAR THE RUMOR
ABOUT BUTTER?

WELL, I'M NOT GOING
TO SPREAD IT!

CAN FEBRUARY
MARCH?

NO, BUT APRIL MAY.

MY WIFE TOLD ME I
HAD TO STOP ACTING
LIKE A FLAMINGO...

SO I HAD TO PUT
MY FOOT DOWN.

IF YOU EVER GET
COLD, JUST STAND IN
A CORNER FOR A BIT...

THEY'RE USUALLY
AROUND 90 DEGREES.

WHAT DO YOU CALL
A SLEEPING BULL?

A BULL-DOZER.

WHAT DID THE
MAGNET SAY TO THE
OTHER MAGNET?

I FIND YOU VERY
ATTRACTIVE!

WHY DID THEY BURY
GEORGE WASHINGTON
STANDING UP?

BECAUSE HE
COULD NEVER LIE.

WHAT IS THE KING
OF ALL INCHES?

THE RULER.

WHY IS THE LETTER
"B" VERY COOL?

BECAUSE IT'S
SITTING IN THE AC.

WHY DID THE MAN
TAKE TOILET PAPER
TO THE PARTY?

BECAUSE HE WAS
A PARTY POOPER.

HOW DO YOU CATCH
A SQUIRREL?

CLIMB A TREE AND
ACT LIKE A NUT.

WHAT DO YOU CALL
A BELT WITH A
WATCH ON IT?

A WAIST OF TIME.

WHY IS ENGLAND THE
WETTEST COUNTRY?

BECAUSE SO MANY
KINGS AND QUEENS
HAVE BEEN
REIGNING THERE.

WHERE DID NOAH
KEEP HIS BEES?

IN HIS ARK HIVES.

WHAT DID THE
JUDGE SAY WHEN A
SKUNK WALKED INTO
THE COURTROOM?

"ODOR IN THE COURT."

WHY ARE VAMPIRES
SO EASY TO FOOL?

BECAUSE THEY
ARE SUCKERS.

WHAT DID THE
FISHERMAN SAY
TO THE MAGICIAN?

PICK A COD, ANY COD.

I WANT TO
GO CAMPING
EVERY YEAR...

THAT TRIP WAS
SO IN TENTS.

WHAT DID THE
BUFFALO SAY TO
HER CHILD AS HE
LEFT FOR SCHOOL?

BISON.

WHAT KIND OF CHEESE
ISN'T YOURS?

NACHO CHEESE.

I'M THINKING
OF BECOMING
A HITMAN...

I HEARD THEY
MAKE A KILLING.

WHY COULDN'T THE KID
SEE THE PIRATE MOVIE?

BECAUSE IT WAS
RATED RRRR.

WHAT GOES
UP AND NEVER
COMES DOWN?

YOUR AGE..

WHAT DO OLYMPIC
SPRINTERS EAT
BEFORE A RACE?

NOTHING THEY FAST.

DID YOU HEAR ABOUT
THE SENSITIVE
BURGLAR?

HE TAKES THINGS
PERSONALLY.

WHERE DOES
THE ELECTRIC CORD
GO TO SHOP?

THE OUTLET MALL.

DID YOU KNOW THE
FIRST FRENCH FRIES
WEREN'T ACTUALLY
COOKED IN FRANCE?

THEY WERE COOKED
IN GREECE.

WHAT'S THE BEST
WAY TO WATCH A FLY
FISHING TOURNAMENT?

LIVE STREAM.

I'VE NEVER GONE TO
A GUN RANGE BEFORE.
I DECIDED TO GIVE
IT A SHOT!

WHAT'S THE
BEST TIME TO GO
TO THE DENTIST?

TOOTH-HURTY.

WHAT DO YOU GET
WHEN YOU CROSS A
SNAKE WITH A PIE?

A PIE-THON.

HOW DO YOU
IMPRESS A
FEMALE BAKER?

BRING HER FLOURS.

WHAT DID THE
SWORDFISH SAY
TO THE MARLIN?

YOU'RE LOOKING
SHARP.

WHAT DO YOU CALL
A ROW OF RABBITS
HOPPING AWAY?

A RECEDING
HARE LINE!

WHY DID THE POLICEMAN
SMELL BAD?

HE WAS ON DUTY.

WHAT'S THE MOST
MUSICAL PART OF
THE CHICKEN?

THE DRUM STICK.

WHY SHOULD YOU
NEVER FALL FOR A
TENNIS PLAYER?

BECAUSE LOVE MEANS
NOTHING TO THEM.

WHAT DO YOU CALL A
PONY WITH A COUGH?

A LITTLE HOARSE.

WHY IS DADDY HUGGING
HIS BARBECUE?

BECAUSE IT IS THE
GRILL OF HIS DREAMS.

I USED TO BE ADDICTED
TO THE HOKEY POKEY...

BUT THEN I TURNED
MYSELF AROUND.

HOW DO YOU MAKE
A SWISS ROLL?

PUSH HIM DOWN
THE MOUNTAIN.

WHY DID THE
STADIUM GET HOT
AFTER THE GAME?

ALL THE FANS LEFT.

WHAT DO YOU CALL
A GUY WHO NEVER
FARTS IN PUBLIC?

A PRIVATE TUTOR.

WHAT DON'T
ANTS GET SICK?

THEY HAVE
ANTY-BODIES.

WORKING IN A
MIRROR FACTORY IS
SOMETHING I CAN
TOTALLY SEE
MYSELF DOING.

WHY COULDN'T THE
SESAME SEED LEAVE
THE CASINO?

BECAUSE HE
WAS ON A ROLL.

WHY DID THE MOBILE
PHONE NEED GLASSES?

IT LOST ALL
ITS CONTACTS.

WHAT DO YOU CALL
TWO FAT PEOPLE
HAVING A CHAT?

A HEAVY DISCUSSION.

WHAT DID THE
JANITOR SAY WHEN
HE JUMPED OUT
OF THE CLOSET?

SUPPLIES!

WHAT DO YOU CALL
A COW WITH
TWO LEGS?

LEAN BEEF.

WHY DIDN'T THE
ASTRONAUT COME
HOME TO HIS WIFE?

HE NEEDED SPACE.

DID YOU HEAR ABOUT
THE POPULATION OF
IRELAND'S CAPITAL?

IT'S DUBLIN.

WHAT DID THE
TRIANGLE SAY
TO THE CIRCLE?

YOU'RE POINTLESS.

WHY DO BIRDS
FLY SOUTH IN
THE WINTER?

BECAUSE IT'S TOO
FAR TO WALK.

IF YOU'RE AMERICAN
IN THE LIVING ROOM,
WHAT ARE YOU IN
THE BATHROOM?

EUROPEAN.

WHICH PET MAKES
THE MOST NOISE?

A TRUMPET.

WHAT DO YOU CALL
A SCARY LOOKING
REINDEER?

A CARIBOO.

WHY WAS TIGGER
LOOKING IN
THE TOILET?

HE WAS LOOKING
FOR POOH.

WHAT DID THE
DUCK SAY TO THE
BARTENDER?

PUT IT ON MY BILL.

WHY DID THE
GOLFER BRING TWO
PAIRS OF PANTS?

IN CASE HE GOT
A HOLE IN ONE.

WHY DID THE
WALRUS GO TO THE
TUPPERWARE PARTY?

HE WAS LOOKING
FOR A TIGHT SEAL.

WHAT DO YOU DO WITH
A DEAD CHEMIST?

YOU BARIUM.

I'M TERRIFIED
OF ELEVATORS...

SO I'M GOING TO
START TAKING STEPS
TO AVOID THEM.

HOW ARE RELATIONSHIPS
A LOT LIKE ALGEBRA?

SOMETIMES YOU
LOOK AT YOUR X
AND WONDERED Y.

HOW DO YOU MAKE A
WITCH ITCH?

TAKE AWAY HER "W."

WHEN DO YOU KNOW
WHEN THE MOON HAS
HAD ENOUGH TO EAT?

WHEN IT'S FULL.

WHY DID THE FISH
GET BAD GRADES?

BECAUSE IT WAS
BELOW SEA LEVEL.

WHAT IS A CLEAN
DESK A SIGN OF?

A VERY FULL
DESK DRAWER.

WHAT DOES THE
MAN IN THE MOON
DO WHEN HIS HAIR
GETS TOO LONG?

ECLIPSE IT.

WHAT DO YOU CALL
SOMEONE WHO
IMMIGRATED
TO SWEDEN?

ARTIFICIAL SWEDENER.

WHAT DID THE TREE
SAY TO THE WIND?

LEAF ME ALONE.

WHAT DID THE HORSE
SAY WHEN HE FELL?

HELP, I'VE FALLEN AND
I CAN'T GIDDY UP!

WHY DID THE
LION EAT THE TIGHT-
ROPE WALKER?

HE WANTED A
WELL-BALANCED MEAL.

YOU WANT TO HEAR
A PIZZA JOKE?

NEVER MIND, IT'S
PRETTY CHEESY.

WHY SHOULD YOU
NEVER LAUGH AT
YOUR SPOUSE'S
CHOICES?

BECAUSE YOU'RE
ONE OF THEM.

WHY DID THE COOKIE
GO TO THE DOCTOR?

BECAUSE HE
FELT CRUMMY.

THERE WERE TWO
PEANUTS WALKING
DOWN A DARK ALLEY,
ONE WAS ASSAULTED.

WHAT DID THE CHIP SAY
WHEN HE SAW THE
CHEESE STEALING?

HEY, THAT'S NACHOS.

WHY DID THE FARMER
HAVE TO SEPARATE
THE CHICKEN AND
THE TURKEY?

HE SENSED FOWL PLAY.

WHAT DID THE HAT
SAY TO THE SCARF?

YOU GO AHEAD, I'LL
HANG AROUND.

WHAT DID THE MAYO SAY
WHEN SOMEONE
OPENED THE
REFRIGERATOR DOOR?

CLOSE THE DOOR,
I AM DRESSING!

WHAT DO YOU CALL
AN ALLIGATOR
IN A VEST?

AN INVESTIGATOR.

WHAT DO YOU CALL
AN ESCAPED OWL?

HOODINI.

WHAT DID THE POLICEMAN
SAY TO HIS BELLY BUTTON?

YOU'RE UNDER A VEST.

WHY DID THE
PIG GET HIRED BY
THE RESTAURANT?

HE WAS REALLY
GOOD AT BACON.

WHY ARE TEDDY
BEARS NEVER
HUNGRY?

BECAUSE THEY'RE
ALWAYS STUFFED.

WHERE DO VOLKSWAGENS
GO WHEN THEY GET OLD?

THE OLD VOLKS HOME.

WHAT'S AN
ASTRONAUT'S
FAVORITE PART
OF A COMPUTER?

THE SPACE BAR.

WHY DOES
SNOOP DOGG USE
AN UMBRELLA?

FOR DIZZLE.

WHAT LIES AT THE
BOTTOM OF THE
SEA SHAKING?

A NERVOUS WRECK.

I'M THINKING ABOUT
REMOVING MY SPINE...

I FEEL LIKE IT'S ONLY
HOLDING ME BACK.

A JUMPER CABLE
WALKS INTO A BAR. THE
BARTENDER SAYS, "I'LL
SERVE YOU, BUT DON'T
START ANYTHING."

COSMETIC SURGERY
USED TO BE SUCH
A TABOO SUBJECT...

NOW YOU CAN TALK ABOUT
BOTOX AND NOBODY
RAISES AN EYEBROW.

DON'T WORRY IF YOU
MISS A GYM SESSION...

EVERYTHING
WILL WORK OUT.

WHAT'S THE STUPIDEST
ANIMAL IN THE JUNGLE?

THE POLAR BEAR.

WHY WAS THE
FOOTBALL COACH
SHAKING THE
VENDING MACHINE?

BECAUSE HE WANTED
HIS QUARTER BACK.

WHAT DID THE CROSS-
EYED TEACHER SAY?

I CAN'T CONTROL
MY PUPILS.

WHERE DO BEES
GO TO THE TOILET?

BP STATION.

HOW DID DARTH VADER
KNOW WHAT LUKE GOT
HIM FOR HIS BIRTHDAY?

HE FELT HIS
PRESENTS.

WHY DID THE SKELETON
CROSS THE ROAD?

TO GET TO THE
BODY SHOP.

WHAT DO YOU CALL BIRDS
THAT STICK TOGETHER?

VEL-CROWS.

IF PILGRIMS WERE
ALIVE TODAY, WHAT
WOULD THEY BE
KNOWN FOR?

THEIR AGE.

WHY DIDN'T THE WITCH
FLY ON HER BROOM
WHEN SHE WAS ANGRY?

SHE WAS AFRAID
SHE WOULD FLY
OFF THE HANDLE.

5/4 OF PEOPLE ADMIT
THAT THEY'RE BAD
WITH FRACTIONS.

HAVE YOU
HEARD ABOUT
THE PREGNANT
BED BUG?

SHE'S GOING TO
HAVE HER BABY
IN THE SPRING.

A COWBOY LEFT
MONTANA TO GO
TO TEXAS ON FRIDAY
AND CAME BACK ON
FRIDAY. HOW DID
HE DO IT?

HE NAMED HIS
HORSE FRIDAY.

CLASS TRIP TO
THE COCA-COLA
FACTORY TODAY...

I HOPE THERE'S
NO POP QUIZ.

A LOT OF PEOPLE CRY
WHEN THEY CUT AN ONION...

THE TRICK IS NOT TO FORM
AN EMOTIONAL BOND.

WHAT DO PRISONERS
USE TO CALL
EACH OTHER?

CELL PHONES.

WHAT STARTS WITH
A P, ENDS WITH AN E,
AND HAS A 1,000
LETTERS?

POST OFFICE.

WHY DID CINDERELLA
GET KICKED OFF THE
SOCCER TEAM?

BECAUSE SHE RAN AWAY
FROM THE BALL.

WHAT DO YOU CALL
A PRETTY GHOST?

BOOTIFUL.

WHAT'S A RACE CAR'S
FAVORITE THING TO
EAT FOR LUNCH?

FAST FOOD.

WHAT DID THE BIG
CHIMNEY SAY TO THE
LITTLE CHIMNEY?

"YOU'RE TOO YOUNG
TO SMOKE."

WHO EARNS A LIVING
BY DRIVING HIS
CUSTOMERS AWAY?

A TAXI DRIVER.

WHY DOES
HUMPTY DUMPTY
LOVE AUTUMN?

BECAUSE HUMPTY
DUMPTY HAD A
GREAT FALL.

WHY CAN'T YOU HEAR
A PTERODACTYL PEE?

BECAUSE THE
"P" IS SILENT.

WHAT NAILS DO CARPENTERS
HATE TO HIT?

FINGERNAILS.

WHY ARE GHOSTS
SUCH GOOD
CHEERLEADERS?

BECAUSE THEY HAVE
A LOT OF SPIRIT.

WANT TO HEAR A
JOKE ABOUT A PIECE
OF PAPER?

NEVERMIND, IT'S
TEARABLE.

IF YOU SEE A ROBBERY
AT AN APPLE STORE
DOES THAT MAKE
YOU AN IWITNESS?

YOU SHOULDN'T KISS
ANYONE ON JANUARY 1ST
BECAUSE IT'S ONLY
THE FIRST DATE.

I WENT TO THE ZOO
AND SAW A BAGUETTE
IN A CAGE.

THE ZOOKEEPER SAID IT
WAS BREAD IN CAPTIVITY!

WHAT DO YOU CALL A
CAN OF SOUP THAT EATS
OTHER CANS OF SOUP?

A CANNIBAL.

I JUST WATCHED A
DOCUMENTARY
ABOUT BEAVERS...

IT WAS THE BEST DAM
SHOW I EVER SAW.

DID YOU HEAR
ABOUT THE GUY WHO
INVENTED LIFESAVERS?

THEY SAY HE
MADE A MINT.

CAN I TELL YOU
A CAT JOKE?

JUST KITTEN!

A HAM SANDWICH WALKS
INTO A BAR AND
ORDERS A BEER...

THE BARTENDER SAYS,
"SORRY WE DON'T SERVE
FOOD HERE."

HOW DO YOU MAKE
HOLY WATER?

YOU BOIL THE
HELL OUT OF IT.

WHAT DO YOU CALL A
COW WITH A TWITCH?

BEEF JERKY.

WHY DO CHICKEN COOPS
ONLY HAVE TWO DOORS?

BECAUSE IF THEY HAD
FOUR, THEY WOULD BE
CHICKEN SEDANS!

WHAT DO
ELVES LEARN IN
KINDERGARTEN?

THE ELF-ABET.

WHAT'S MORE AMAZING
THAN A TALKING DOG?

A SPELLING BEE.

WHY DID THE CLYDESDALE
GIVE THE PONY A GLASS
OF WATER?

BECAUSE HE WAS
A LITTLE HORSE.

I HAD A DREAM THAT
I WAS A MUFFLER
LAST NIGHT...

I WOKE UP EXHAUSTED.

WHAT DO YOU CALL
A LONELY CHEESE?

PROVOLONE.

WHY DIDN'T THE
VAMPIRE ATTACK
TAYLOR SWIFT?

SHE HAD
BAD BLOOD.

WHAT DO YOU GET
WHEN YOU CROSS
A SNOWMAN WITH
A VAMPIRE?

FROSTBITE.

WHAT DOES A ZOMBIE
VEGETARIAN EAT?

"GRRRAAAAAIIIINNNNS!"

I WAS INTERROGATED
OVER THE THEFT OF
A CHEESE TOASTIE...

MAN, THEY REALLY
GRILLED ME.

WHAT DO YOU CALL
SOMEONE WITH NO
BODY AND NO NOSE?

NOBODY KNOWS.

WHAT IS RED AND SMELLS
LIKE BLUE PAINT?

RED PAINT.

WHERE DID
THE COLLEGE-AGED
VAMPIRE LIKE
TO SHOP?

FOREVER 21.

WHY DID THE
CARPENTER LEAVE
THE LUMBER STORE?

BECAUSE HE
GOT BORED.

RIP BOILED WATER...

YOU WILL BE MIST.

YOU HEARD OF THAT
NEW BAND 1023MB?

THEY'RE GOOD BUT
THEY HAVEN'T GOT
A GIG YET.

A FURNITURE STORE
KEEPS CALLING ME...

ALL I WANTED WAS
ONE NIGHT STAND.

I DON'T TRUST STAIRS...

THEY'RE ALWAYS UP
TO SOMETHING.

I WAS GOING TO TELL
A JOKE ABOUT DOGS...

BUT I FELT IT WAS A
LITTLE FAR-FETCHED.

WHY IS YOUR NOSE
IN THE MIDDLE OF
YOUR FACE?

BECAUSE IT'S
THE SCENTER.

TO THE GUY WHO
INVENTED THE ZERO...

THANKS FOR NOTHING.

I SOLD MY VACUUM
CLEANER...

IT WAS JUST
GATHERING DUST.

DID YOU HEAR
THAT ARNOLD
SCHWARZENEGGER
WILL BE DOING A
MOVIE ABOUT
CLASSICAL MUSIC?

HE'LL BE BACH.

WHY DID THE BARBER
WIN THE RACE?

HE KNEW A SHORTCUT.

MY FRIEND KEEPS
SAYING "CHEER UP MAN
IT COULD BE WORSE,
YOU COULD BE STUCK
UNDERGROUND IN A
HOLE FULL OF WATER..."

I KNOW HE MEANS WELL.

THE DIFFERENCE
BETWEEN A NUMERATOR
AND A DENOMINATOR
IS A SHORT LINE...

ONLY A FRACTION
OF PEOPLE WILL
UNDERSTAND THIS.

COOKING OUT THIS
WEEKEND? DON'T
FORGET THE PICKLE...

IT'S KIND OF A BIG DILL.

WHAT DO YOU CALL A
MAN WITH NO ARMS OR
LEGS IN THE MIDDLE
OF THE OCEAN?

BOB.

WHAT IS THE COLOR
OF THE WIND?

BLEW.

I'LL DO ALGEBRA,
TACKLE GEOMETRY,
MAYBE EVEN A
LITTLE CALCULUS...

BUT GRAPHING IS
WHERE I DRAW
THE LINE.

HOW DOES A PENGUIN
BUILD ITS HOUSE?

IGLOOS IT TOGETHER!

WHICH REINDEER
LIKES TO CLEAN?

COMET.

THE INVENTOR OF THE
THROAT LOZENGE
HAS DIED...

THERE WILL BE NO
COFFIN AT HIS FUNERAL.

HOW MUCH DID
THE PIRATE'S NEW
EARRINGS COST HIM?

A BUCCANEER.

WHAT DID THE GRAPE
DO WHEN HE GOT
STEPPED ON?

HE LET OUT A LITTLE WINE.

WHAT DO YOU CALL
A FACTORY THAT
MAKES GOOD
PRODUCTS?

A SATIS-FACTORY.

WHAT DO YOU
CALL A MAN THAT
IRONS CLOTHES?

IRON MAN.

WHAT DO YOU CALL
A BABY MONKEY?

A CHIMP OFF
THE OLD BLOCK.

I HAVE KLEPTOMANIA...

SOMETIMES WHEN IT
GETS REALLY BAD, I
TAKE SOMETHING FOR IT.

WHAT STAYS IN
ONE CORNER BUT
TRAVELS AROUND
THE WORLD?

A STAMP.

HAD SEAFOOD
LAST NIGHT...

NOW I'M EEL.

HOW IS CHRISTMAS
LIKE YOUR JOB?

YOU DO ALL THE WORK
AND THE FAT GUY IN
THE SUIT GETS ALL
THE CREDIT.

WHEN YOU HAVE A
BLADDER INFECTION...

URINE TROUBLE.

HAVE YOU HEARD ABOUT
THE NEW BROOM?

IT'S SWEEPING THE NATION.

WHAT TYPE OF
DIET DID THE
SNOWMAN GO ON?

THE MELTDOWN DIET.

WHY DID THE POOR
MAN SELL YEAST?

TO RAISE SOME
DOUGH.

WHY DID FROSTY ASK
FOR A DIVORCE?

HIS WIFE WAS A
TOTAL FLAKE.

HOW DO YOU DROWN
A HIPSTER?

IN THE MAINSTREAM.

I'M THINKING ABOUT
GETTING A NEW
HAIRCUT...

I'M GOING TO
MULLET OVER.

WHAT DO YOU CALL
A ROW OF PEOPLE
LIFTING MOZZARELLA?

A CHEESY PICK UP LINE.

MY WIFE ACCUSED ME
OF BEING IMMATURE...

I TOLD HER TO GET
OUT OF MY FORT.

PARALLEL LINES
HAVE SO MUCH
IN COMMON...

IT'S A SHAME THEY'LL
NEVER MEET.

TWO GUYS WALK
INTO A BAR...

THE THIRD
ONE DUCKS.

I ATE A CLOCK
YESTERDAY...

IT WAS VERY TIME
CONSUMING.

PEOPLE DON'T LIKE
HAVING TO BEND OVER
TO GET THEIR DRINKS.

WE REALLY NEED TO
RAISE THE BAR.

I THOUGHT ABOUT
GOING ON AN ALL-
ALMOND DIET....

BUT THAT'S JUST NUTS!

WHY DO SEAGULLS
FLY OVER THE SEA?

BECAUSE IF THEY
FLEW OVER THE BAY,
THEY WOULD BE
CALLED BAGLES.

WHAT DID THE BOY
VOLCANO SAY TO THE
GIRL VOLCANO?

I LAVA YOU.

WHAT DO YOU CALL
A FAT PSYCHIC?

A FOUR CHIN TELLER.